First World War
and Army of Occupation
War Diary
France, Belgium and Germany

30 DIVISION
Divisional Troops
226 Machine Gun Company
11 July 1917 - 28 February 1918

WO95/2323/6

The Naval & Military Press Ltd
www.nmarchive.com
Published in association with The National Archives

Published by

The Naval & Military Press Ltd

Unit 10 Ridgewood Industrial Park,

Uckfield, East Sussex,

TN22 5QE England

Tel: +44 (0) 1825 749494

www.naval-military-press.com

www.nmarchive.com

This diary has been reprinted in facsimile from the original. Any imperfections are inevitably reproduced and the quality may fall short of modern type and cartographic standards.

© **Crown Copyright**
Images reproduced by permission of The National Archives, London, England, 2015.

Contents

Document type	Place/Title	Date From	Date To
Heading	WO95/2323/6 30th Divisional Divl Troops 220th Machine Gun Coy 1917 July-1918 Feb		
Heading	30th Division Divl Troops From U K 226th Machine Gun Coy. 1917 July-1918 Feb		
Heading	War Diary 226th Machine Gun Coy Month Of August 1917 Sept 19		
War Diary	Southampton Le Havre	11/07/1917	18/07/1917
War Diary	Hopoutre	19/07/1917	19/07/1917
War Diary	Steenvoorde	20/07/1917	22/07/1917
War Diary	Ouderdom	23/07/1917	05/08/1917
War Diary	Steenvoorde	06/08/1917	07/08/1917
War Diary	Merris	08/08/1917	11/08/1917
War Diary	Westoutre	12/08/1917	23/08/1917
War Diary	Dranoutre	24/08/1917	31/08/1917
War Diary	Ouderdom	02/08/1917	03/08/1917
War Diary	Dranoutre	01/09/1917	31/10/1917
Heading	War Diary Of 226th Company, Machine Gun Corps, For The Month Of November, 1917. Volume No. 1 Vol 5		
War Diary	Dranoutre	01/11/1917	16/11/1917
War Diary	Oudezeele	17/11/1917	26/11/1917
War Diary	Reninghelst	27/11/1917	30/11/1917
Heading	War Diary Of The 226th Company, Machine Gun Corps For The Month Of December 1917 Volume No Capt D.A.A.G. 30th Division Volume 6		
War Diary	Reninghelst	01/12/1917	31/12/1917
Heading	War Diary Of The 226th Company, Machine Gun Corps. For The Month Of January 1918 Volume No. 7 Capt D.A.A.G. 30th Division.		
War Diary	Reninghelst	01/01/1918	07/01/1918
War Diary	Blaringham	08/01/1918	11/01/1918
War Diary	Hamelet	12/01/1918	13/01/1918
War Diary	Harbonnieres	14/01/1918	18/01/1918
War Diary	Saulchoy	19/01/1918	19/01/1918
War Diary	Fretoy	20/01/1918	26/01/1918
War Diary	Baboeuf	27/01/1918	31/01/1918
Heading	War Diary. Of The 226th Company Machine Gun Corps. For The Month Of February 1918 Volume No. 1		
War Diary	Marizele	01/02/1918	09/02/1918
War Diary	Bourguignon	10/02/1918	10/02/1918
War Diary	Guiscard	11/02/1918	11/02/1918
War Diary	Esmery-Hallon	12/02/1918	21/02/1918
War Diary	Douchy	22/02/1918	28/02/1918

WO 95/2323/6

30th Divisional Div Troops

226TH MACHINE Gun COY

1917 JULY — 1918 FEB

30TH DIVISION
DIVL TROOPS

From UK

226TH MACHINE GUN COY.
~~AND 30 BN. MGC~~
~~AUG 1917 SEP 1918~~

1917 JULY — 1918 FEB

Dan Lorimer Cushing San Cory Assent
226 Machins Ct
month 1977

Sep 15

ORIGINAL

226 MG Coy
Vol I

WAR DIARY
or
INTELLIGENCE SUMMARY.

(Erase heading not required.)

Army Form C. 2118.

Instructions regarding War Diaries and Intelligence Summaries are contained in F.S. Regs., Part II. and the Staff Manual respectively. Title pages will be prepared in manuscript.

Place	Date	Hour	Summary of Events and Information	Remarks and references to Appendices
SOUTHAMPTON	11/4/17	5 PM	Embarked on S.S. "NORTH WEST MILLER" left Southampton about 9 P.M.	
LE HAVRE	12/4/17	6 AM	Reached port. Proceeded to No.1 Rest Camp. Section A arriving about 9 P.M. M.K.B.	
"	13/4/17		In Rest Camp. O.R. Casualties 2 sick (received) M.K.B.	
"	14/4/17		" Received 4 mules from No. 2 Base Remounts M.K.B.	
"	15/4/17		" M.K.B.	
"	16/4/17		" O.R. Casualties 2 from Hospital (increase) M.K.B.	
"	17/4/17		" M.K.B.	
"	18/4/17	10.30PM	Marched out of Rest Camp. Entrained on Round 13 Aug 1.30 P.M – 2 P.M left LE HAVRE M.K.B	
HOPOUTRE	19/4/17	11 AM	Detrained and marched to STEENVOORDE (10 Kilos) arriving 4 P.M – attached 30th Division M.K.B	
STEENVOORDE	20/4/17		At rest in billets. Casualties 1 O.R. sick (received) M.K.B	
"	21/4/17		" Inspection by G.O.C. M.K.B	
"	22/4/17	1 PM	Marched out. Arrived OUDERDOM 5.30 P.M. "B" Section relieved one section of 54 M.G.Coy in 90th M.G. Coy. One section duty by 6.30 P.M – "C" Section 4.32 O.R marched out at midnight to the trenches	
OUDERDOM	23/4/17		At rest. Aircraft duty by the line Junction (CORNWALL camp) M.K.B	
"	24/4/17		At rest in Ederhall camp. "C" Coy reconnoitred gun positions for a barrage to the fixed Shelly Canadas 2ND LIEUT F.H. MATTHEWS MILLER 2ND R.I DEAN wounded when route to trenches (all shell-fire) 1 O.R. Sics (½ CCS) M.K.B	
"	25/4/17	6 PM	"C" Section joining up gun positions near MAPLE COPSE M.K.13	
"	26/4/17	6 PM	"C" Section withdrawn from MAPLE COPSE. M.K.B on the 2 Officers and 29 Other ranks relieved from instruction trenches M.K.13	
"	28/4/17	6.30PM	1 SubSection F.H. Midder 2nd Lt I.R.B. N'rksal front up gun positions at Granville Batty M.K.13	
"	29/4/17	10.30PM	Guns on Anti Aircraft duty fired about 1200 rounds at E.A's. M.K.13	
"	30/4/17	10.30PM	Fine weather today. Heavy rain at intervals M.K.13	
"	30/4/17	7PM	No rest. Aircraft duty by the line Junction. A/B	
			Company duty @ Rest Section + "B" Section deployed out for each as ordered M.K.B.	

Wilfred Cpt
OC 226 Coy M.G.C

WAR DIARY or INTELLIGENCE SUMMARY

Army Form C. 2118.

Instructions regarding War Diaries and Intelligence Summaries are contained in F.S. Regs., Part II. and the Staff Manual respectively. Title pages will be prepared in manuscript.

(Erase heading not required.)

ORIGINAL

Place	Date	Hour	Summary of Events and Information	Remarks and references to Appendices
OUDERDOM.	1/8/17	2 p.m.	Company returned from Chateau SEGARD. Casualty 1 O.R. returned from 2.S.F.A. (Increase)	A.F.K.13.
"	2/8/17	3 A.M.	"C" Section relieved "B" Section on A.A. duty, and "A" Sub Section relieved O.K. "A" Sub section	
		5 A.M.	One Sub Section of "A" Section, and "B" Section marched out to be repositions near DORMY HOUSE and MAPLE COPSE.	
		9.30 A.M.	"D" Section marched out to DORMY HOUSE	
			with 2/Lt MORISON marched out to 89th route and commenced re A.A. duty and strengthening the line near WELLINGTON CRESCENT. "B" Section with 2nd Lt. HOUGHTON marched out for A.A. duty W.K.6, group RSA. "D" Section, 2nd Lt HUNT marched out to 21 Inf bde and were issued CRNS CRAYL guns which 1 gun team were	
	3/8/17	11 A.M.	sent to advanced gun position where SGA Rumsey was killed (missing) 2 signing party killed (missing). Casualties: Killed (O.Rs.) 1, wounded 1, missing 1. "D" Section returned to OUDERDOM.	A.F.K.8.
	4/8/17		"A" Sub Section + "B" Section 2nd Lts R.B.CONGDON and W.H. CURTIS and 3 other ranks reported A.H.G. Reinforcements. Company at rest.	A.F.K.13
	5/8/17	9 A.M.	"A" Sub Section + "C" Section relieved on A.A. duty by 218 M.G. Coy.	
		p.m.	Remained flog. untrained in alteration and Sub Sn. detrained at CHESTRE and bussed to STEENVOORDE. 9.45 A.M. Transport marched out for STEENVOORDE A.F.K.8.	
STEENVOORDE	6/8/17		Company at rest. Stores checked for re-fitting. Company attached to 39th Bn. for administration etc.	
	7/8/17	10 A.M.	Marched to MERRIS A.F.K.13	
MERRIS	8/8/17		Company at rest. Clothes checked for re-fitting etc. C.B.	
	9/8/17		2 Sub Sections of "D" Section with 2nd Lts. HUNT and CURTIS released M.G. gun A.A. duty at M34 A.R and S27 C. 6.49 pm	
	10/8/17		2/Lt BULLEN accidentally.	A.F.K.B.
	11/8/17		Company at rest	A.F.K.8
	12/8/17		Marched to M.42.27 near WESTOUTRE, arrived 12.25 p.m.	A.F.K.8.
WESTOUTRE	13/8/17		At rest A.F.K.B. G.O.B. A.F.K.8	
"	14/8/17	1 P.M.	2/Lt HUNT and 1 Sub section returned from A.A. Duty at LOCRE CHATEAU Dugout H.F.13	
"	15/8/17	11 A.M.	Inspection by G.O.C, 2 Army A.F.K.8	
"	16/8/17		At rest A.F.K.B.	
"	17/8/17		At rest A.F.K.	
"	18/8/17		At rest A.F.K.	
"	19/8/17		At rest A.F.K.B.	
"	20/8/17		At rest	A.F.K.8

Army Form C. 2118.

WAR DIARY
or
INTELLIGENCE SUMMARY.
(Erase heading not required.)

ORIGINAL

Instructions regarding War Diaries and Intelligence Summaries are contained in F. S. Regs., Part II. and the Staff Manual respectively. Title pages will be prepared in manuscript.

Place	Date	Hour	Summary of Events and Information	Remarks and references to Appendices
WESTOUTRE	21/8/17		At rest. Company Sports. MK13.	
"	22/8/17		At rest. MK10.	
"	23/8/17	9.5 a.m.	Marched to DRANOUTRE 35.a.95. 2 0 p.m. 2/Lt. H.R.V.H.HUNT took SubSection "D" sent on 2/Lt. Section O.4. H.Q. 30th Divn. at 35.C.4.8 2/Lt. J.A.WARDLE to 98th FA (Tank) evacuated to 53 C.C.S. MK13.	
DRANOUTRE	24/8/17	7 p.m.	2/Lt. R.B.CONGDON and 1 SubSection "C" proceeded to AH duty at BAY FARM. H.2.d.8.6.	
		7 p.m.	2/Lt. M. HOUGHTON and "B" Section to ANZAC FARM 28.a.2.0. using harassing fire at night on enemy trenches, firing about 10,000 rounds per night. MK13.	
"	25/8/17		No change. MK13.	
"	26/8/17		2/Lt. R.B. MORISON proceeded to IX Corps Infantry School, BERTHEN for 1 month's course. MK13. Lce/Cpl J.A.WARDLE to Lce/S. MK13.	
"	27/8/17	10 a.m.	"C" SubSection in camp relieved "D" SubSection on AH duty at D.S.T. H.Q. 2/Lt. H.R.V.H.HUNT relieved 2/Lt. W.H.CURTIS at TRENT DUMP. "D" B Section at D.S.T. H.Q. returned to camp.	
"	28/8/17	9 p.m.	2/Lt. CURTIS joined 2nd Lt. R.B.CONGDON at BAY FARM. 11 p.m. 2nd Lt. A. DONALDSON and "A" Section relieved 2nd Lt. T.M. HOUGHTON and "B" Section at ANZAC FARM and also took on S.O.S. lines of fire for Divisional defence Scheme. MK13.	
"	29/8/17		No change. MK13.	
"	30/8/17	12 h.	2/Lt. T.M. HOUGHTON + Sub Section of B relieved 2/Lt. H.R.V.H.HUNT + SubSection of D at TRENT DUMP. SubSection of B relieved SubSection of C at D.S.T. H.Q. DRANOUTRE.	
"	31/8/17	5 p.m.	2nd Lt. R.B. CONGDON returned from BAY FARM having handed over to 2 Lt. W.H. CURTIS. MK13.	MK13.
		6 p.m.	2/Lt. R. PRENTICE reported from Base. MK13.	

H.V.Curt Capt.

O.C. 228 M.G.Coy

Army Form C. 2118.

WAR DIARY
or
INTELLIGENCE SUMMARY.
(Erase heading not required.)

Instructions regarding War Diaries and Intelligence Summaries are contained in F. S. Regs., Part II. and the Staff Manual respectively. Title pages will be prepared in manuscript.

Place	Date	Hour	Summary of Events and Information	Remarks and references to Appendices
			Sept 1st 1917	
OUDERDOM	2/8/17	10 a.m.	AMMENDMENT TO ~~JULY~~ AUGUST 1917 DIARY	
			for "D" Section, 2nd Lt HUNT marched out ..... read "D" Section, under Sgt WESTON marched out."	
			Insert	
OUDERDOM	3/8/17	11.30 a.m.	2nd Lt HUNT, who had been ~~sent~~ on RR duty with 2nd Lt HOUGHTON took over D Section at CRAB CRAWL A/C Boyle. Capt. Forms/C.2118/13 O.C. 226 MG Coy	

ORIGINAL

226 M.G. Coy

Vol 3

Army Form C. 2118.

WAR DIARY
or
INTELLIGENCE SUMMARY.
(Erase heading not required.)

Instructions regarding War Diaries and Intelligence Summaries are contained in F.S. Regs., Part II. and the Staff Manual respectively. Title pages will be prepared in manuscript.

Place	Date	Hour	Summary of Events and Information	Remarks and references to Appendices
DRANOUTRE	1/9/17	9 p.m.	Sgt TULLEY & Sub-Section relieved Sgt NIELD & Sub-Section at BAY FARM. 2nd Lt W.H. CURTIS remained in charge	MK13
"	2/9/17	11.30 a.m.	2nd Lt HOUGHTON & Sub-Section of TRENT DUMP relieved by 226 M.G. Coy.	
"		11.30 p.m.	2nd Lt H.R.V.H. HUNT & "D" Section relieved "B" Section 1 Sub-Section 247 Coy. at O.15.d.	MK13
"	3/9/17	6 p.m.	2nd Lt HUNT visits up positions at O.21.w 3.1 (Sec H.Q.) from O.21.a w 31cd. "A" Section relieved by 21st M.G. Coy.	
"		9 p.m.	Advanced Coy. H.R. established at LEG COPSE. Sgt NIELD & sub Section co-operated in barrage with... LINE.	MK13
"		9 p.m.	2nd Lt W.H. CURTIS and BAY FARM, making total of 8 guns in or east of Y ...... LINE.	MK13
"	4/9/17		H.Q. "C" + "D" Sections in the trenches.	MK13
"	5/9/17		" " " " " " "	MK13
"	6/9/17		" " " " " " "	MK13
"	7/9/17		" " " " " " "	MK13
"	8/9/17		" " " " " " "	MK13
"	9/9/17		" " " " " " "	MK13
"	10/9/17		"B" Section with 2nd Lt T.M. HOUGHTON & 2nd Lt R.B. CONGDON relieved "D" Section. "D" Section with 2nd Lt H.R.V.H. HUNT, relieved "C" Section. "C" Section with 2nd Lt W.H. CURTIS withdrawn to DRANOUTRE.	
"	11/9/17		"A" Sub Section, with Sgt. SPENCER, attached to "B" Section took over from 90 M.G. Coy. 2 gun position at OOSTAVERNE	MK13
"	12/9/17		"H.Q." "B" and "D" Section, one sub-section "A" in the trenches.	MK13
"	13/9/17		" " " " " " "	MK13
"	14/9/17		" " " " " " "	MK13
"	15/9/17		" " " " " " "	MK13
"	16/9/17		" " " " " " "	MK13
"	17/9/17		" " " " " " "	MK13
"	18/9/17		"C" Section with 2nd Lt W.H. CURTIS relieved "B" Section. "B" Section relieved "D" Section with 2nd Lt H.R.V.H. HUNT returned to DRANOUTRE. Lt A. Donaldson took over "A" Sub Section from 2nd Lt R.B. CONGDON in the trenches.	MK13
"	19/9/17		2nd Lt T.M. HOUGHTON returned to DRANOUTRE. 2nd Lt R.B. CONGDON remained in charge of "B" Section at K.B.	MK13
"	20/9/17	5.45 a.m.	W.A. DONALDSON with "A" sub Section Co-operated in 2nd Army attack by engaging BANG FARM from Shellhole line.	MK13
"		3 p.m.	Lt A. DONALDSON to 46 R Field Ambulance.	MK13

J.R. Gray Capt OC 226 Coy. MLC

WAR DIARY or INTELLIGENCE SUMMARY.

Army Form C. 2118.

Place	Date	Hour	Summary of Events and Information	Remarks and references to Appendices
DRANOUTRE	21/9/17		Lt. A. DONALDSON evacuated to 1st Aust. C.C.S. 2nd Lt. T.M. HOUGHTON relieved 2nd Lt. R.B. CONGDON who returned to DRANOUTRE. 2nd Lt. W.H. PRENTICE took over "A" Sub Section in the trenches. App. B	
"	22/9/17		2nd Lt. R.B. MORISON returned from IX Corps School. Casualties 1 O.R. killed. 2 O.R. wounded. App. B	
"	23/9/17		No change. App. B	
"	24/9/17		2nd Lt. R.B. MORISON joined 2nd Lt. R. PRENTICE with "A" Sub Section App.K.B.	
"	25/9/17		2nd Lt. R.B. CONGDON reported to IX Corps Infantry School App.B	
"	26/9/17		"D" Section with 2nd Lt. HUNT relieved "C" Section under 2nd Lt. T.M. HOUGHTON. "B" returned to DRANOUTRE. 2nd Lt. R.B. MORISON took over "A" Sub Section in the trenches from 2nd Lt. R. PRENTICE who joined "D" Section. App.K.B	
"	27/9/17		HQ, "A" Sub Section "C" and "D" Sections in the trenches App.C.B	
"	28/9/17		" " " " App.C B	
"	29/9/17		" " " " App.C.B	
"	30/9/17		" " " " App.C.B	

WAR DIARY or INTELLIGENCE SUMMARY

Army Form C. 2118.

226 M.G. Coy Vol 17

Place	Date	Hour	Summary of Events and Information	Remarks and references to Appendices
DRANOUTRE	1/10/17		HQ, one sub section "A", and "C" - "D" Sections in the line. 2nd Lt. T.M. HOUGHTON returned from R.F.A. Course (148 B. RFA) M which he had proceeded 30/9/17.	
"	2/10/17	5.30p.m.	Guns of "C" Section at D.27.B.2.4 withdrawn - Guns of "C" section at D.27.B.00.65 relieved by 21st M.G. by. One sub section "C" returned to camp. 2nd Lt A.T. O'REGAN 2nd Lt R.B. CONDON medilled from "IX" Corps. Infantry School at BERTHEN. 2nd Lt R. PRENTICE	
"	3/10/17	8.30p.m.	"A" sub-section relieved "C" sub-section at Nr. B.5.4 position 2nd Lt W.H. CURTIS and "C" sub-section out. Into to camp. M.K.B.	
"	4/10/17		HQ, "A" & "D" sections in the line. 2nd Lt R. PRENTICE joins unit "D" Section in the line. M.K.B. "B" Section with 2nd Lt T.M. HOUGHTON, 2nd Lt R.B. CONDON, 35 OR's make up a complete transport taking up positions near Rd to DOULIEU in readiness for entrainment (proceeding East). M.K.B.	
"	5/10/17		HQ "A" & "D" Sections in the line. M.K.B.	
"	6/10/17		"B" Section (2nd Lt T.M. HOUGHTON, 2nd Lt R.B. CONDON) entrained at LAGORGUE and arrived	
"	7/10/17	8.30 p.m.	Strength of 226 M.G. by 12.10 a.m. to 11 a.m. 6000 rounds fired by B guns on S.O.S. left but section in defence.	
"	8/10/17		HQ "A" & "D" Sections in the line. M.K.B. to S.O.S. call. M.K.B.	
"	9/10/17	9 p.m.	"A" Sub-section at OOTATAERNE relieved by 89 M.G. Coy. "A" Sub Section, 2nd Lt R.B. MORISON returned to Camp. Guns of "A" sub-section in O.21.d 05.55 withdrawn and put in the line at D.27.b.00.65, relieving guns of 21st M.G. by. or Rest position. M.K.B.	
"	10/10/17		2nd Lt R.B. MORISON proceeded to RFA Course in the line with 148 Bde RFA.	
"	11/10/17	7.30 p.m.	"C" Section with 2nd Lt W.H. CURTIS relieved "D" Section. 2nd Lt H R.V.H. HINT & 2nd Lt R. PRENTICE who returned to camp. M.K.B.	
"	12/10/17		HQ, A Sub-section and "C" in the line. 2nd Lt A.J. O'REGAN returned to camp after 3 of stage Baths & pledic. M.K.B.	
"	13/10/17		" " " 2nd Lt R.B. MORISON returned from RFA Course. 2 Lt R. PRENTICE proceeded to 148th	
"	14/10/17		Bde RFA for 4 days course in the line Bn. 2nd Lt A.J. O'REGAN returned to the line M.K.B. 14/10/17 not returned (illeg) bombed 14/10/17 M.K.B.	14/10/17
"	15/10/17		HQ "A" sub section + "C" in the line M.K.B.	
"	16/10/17	7 p.m.	Capt F.B. CRAIG proceeded to U.K. on leave; Capt H.K. BOYLE assumed command of the Company. A sub section "A" in the line relieved by A sub Section in camp and returned to camp. M.K.B. Night harassing fire commenced with barrage guns in co-operation with the Artillery M.K.B.	
"	17/10/17		HQ, A Sub Section and "C" in the line. M.K.B. 2nd Lt R. PRENTICE returned from and Lt A McCOLL proceed to R.F.A. course in the field with 148th Bde R.F.A. M.K.B.	

WAR DIARY or INTELLIGENCE SUMMARY

Army Form C. 2118.

Place	Date	Hour	Summary of Events and Information	Remarks and references to Appendices
DRANOUTRE	18/10/17	7p.m.	"D" Section 2nd Lt H.R.V.H.HUNT relieved "C" Section. 2nd Lt. W.H. CURTIS in the line. MFB.	
"	19/10/17		HQ, "A" Sub Section + "D" in the line. MFB.	
"	20/10/17		6 p.m. 2nd Lt. R.B. MORISON relieved 2nd Lt. A.J. O'REGAN in charge of "A" Sub Section. MM.	
"	21/10/17		" " " " . 2nd Lt. A.J. O'REGAN proceeded to R.F.A. Course in the field with 148th Bde R.F.A.	
		7p.m.	Lt. A. McCOLL returned from and 2nd Lt. W.H. CURTIS proceeded to R.F.A. Course in the field with 148th Bde R.F.A.	
"	22/10/17		"A" No 1 Sub Section relieved No 2 Sub Section which returned to Camp. MFB.	
"	23/10/17		HQ, "A" 1 Sub Section + "D" in the line. MFB.	
"	24/10/17		Corps Commander inspected HQ. MFB.	
"	25/10/17	8p.m.	"C" Section relieved "D" section which returned to Camp. 2nd Lt H.R.V.H. HUNT took charge of "C" Sec. in the line. MFB.	
"	26/10/17		2nd Lt W.H. CURTIS returned from + 2nd Lt. A.J. O'REGAN proceeded to R.F.A. Course in the field with 148th Bde R.F.A. MFB.	
"	27/10/17		HQ. "A" 1 Sub Sec + "C" in the line. 6 p.m. "A" 2 Sub Section proceeded to ULSTER HQ as working party. Rd. A. McColl proceeded to 0-21.c.9.3. MFB.	
			"A" 2 Sub Section seen up into the line to build and dug out the new line at 0-21.c.9.3. MFB.	
"	28/10/17		Capt. F.B. CRAIG returned from U.K. and resumed Command of the Company. 2/Lt H.R.V.H. HUNT proceeded to 2/Lt. A.J. O'REGAN returned from R.F.A. Course. A Sub Sect. Relieved A1 Sub Sect. by whole returning to Camp.	
"	29/10/17		"B" Sect. Relieves "C" Sect. which returned to Camp. + 2/Lt. W.H. CURTIS returning in its stead.	
"	30/10/17			
"	31/10/17		HQ. "A" 2 Sub Section + "D" in the line. MFB.	

J.M. Craig Capt.
225th Company monckhope Area
E. Suto.

SECRET.　　　　　WAR DIARY

　　　　　　of 226th Company, Machine Gun Corps,

　　　　　　for the month of November, 1917.

　　　　　　　　VOLUME NO. 1.

ORIGINAL

Army Form C. 2118.

WAR DIARY
or
INTELLIGENCE SUMMARY.
(Erase heading not required.)

Instructions regarding War Diaries and Intelligence Summaries are contained in F.S. Regs., Part II. and the Staff Manual respectively. Title pages will be prepared in manuscript.

Place	Date	Hour	Summary of Events and Information	Remarks and references to Appendices
DRANOUTRE	1/11/17		HQ, "A2" & "D" Sections in the line.	
"	2/11/17		12 men from South Wales Regt. attached to 226 Coy. for duty	
"	3/11/17	10.A.M.	2nd Lt. A.T. O'REGAN relieved 2nd Lt. R.B. MORISON in charge of A subsection in the line. Capt. H.K. BOYLE proceeded on leave to U.K.	2nd Lt Hunt return from RFA course having given up decision to enter RFC
		7 P.M.	"A1" Sub section relieved "A2" which returned to Camp. HQ, "A1" and "D" Sections in the line.	
"	4/11/17			
"	5/11/17		2nd Lt. R.B. MORISON and 4 O.R. proceeded to 42nd Squadron, R.F.C., for A.A. Course.	
"	6/11/17		6.30 pm "C" Section relieved "D" Section which returned to Camp; 2nd Lt. H.R.V.H.	
"	7/11/17		Lt. A. McCOLL returned from U.K. HUNT remained in charge of "C" Section.	
"	8/11/17		HQ, "A1" and "C" Sections in the line. Transport lines moved to D.A.C. Transport lines on the DRANOUTRE - BAILLEUL road.	
"	9/11/17		2nd Lt. W.H. CURTIS relieved 2nd Lt. H.R.V.H. HUNT in charge of "C" Section.	
"	10/11/17	6.45 pm	"A2" Subsection relieved "A1" Sub section in the line.	
"	11/11/17		HQ, "A2" and "C" Sections in the line. OC Coy 14th Australian M.G. Coy made preliminary reconnaissance of line.	
"	12/11/17		2nd Lt. R.B. MORISON and 4 O.R. returned from 42nd Squadron, R.F.C.; HQ, A2 & "C" Sections in the line.	
"	13/11/17		The Company in the line relieved by 14th Australian Machine Gun Company.	
"	14/11/17		Company went to rest at DRANOUTRE.	
"	15/11/17		2nd Lt. H.R.V.H. HUNT proceeded to U.K. on leave.	
"	16/11/17	8 a.m.	Company proceeded to OUDEZEELE, personnel by bus, transport by road.	
OUDEZEELE	17/11/17		Company in rest at OUDEZEELE	
"	18/11/17		"	
"	19/11/17		"	
"	20/11/17		"	
"	21/11/17		" Capt. H.K. BOYLE reported to Company from U.K.	
"	22/11/17		"	
"	23/11/17		" Capt. F.B. CRAIG, 2nd Lt. A. T'O'REGAN, and R. PRENTICE proceeded to STIRLING CASTLE to reconnoitre gun positions and returned same day.	
"	24/11/17		Company in rest at OUDEZEELE. 2/Lt R.B. MORISON to 44 C.C.S.	
"	25/11/17			
"	26/11/17	9 am	9am 2/Lt Prentice + 6 or proceeded into the line. D Section 2/Lt F. Prentice were attached to 89 M.G. Coy with 6 guns. + relieved 6 guns of 220 M.G. Coy. Remainder of Company moved to M.S.C.126 near RENINGHELST.	

A 5834 Wt. W 4973/M687 750,000 8/16 D.D. & I. Ltd. Forms/C.2118/13

ORIGINAL

Army Form C. 2118.

WAR DIARY
or
INTELLIGENCE SUMMARY.
(Erase heading not required.)

Instructions regarding War Diaries and Intelligence Summaries are contained in F. S. Regs., Part II. and the Staff Manual respectively. Title pages will be prepared in manuscript.

Place	Date	Hour	Summary of Events and Information	Remarks and references to Appendices
RENINGHELST	27-11-17		D. Section in the line.	
"	28-11-17		D " " "	
"	29-11-17		Capt. F.B. CRAIG slightly wounded. Capt. H.K. Boyle to assumed command of the company. 2Lt R.B. MORISON returned from 44th to 2.C.B.	
"	30.11.17		D. Section in the line.	

"Secret"

War Diary

of the 226th Company, Machine Gun Corps.

for the month of December 1917

Volume No

(Sgd) Capt
D.a.a.G. 30th Division

2/1/18.

WAR DIARY or INTELLIGENCE SUMMARY

Army Form C. 2118.

Place	Date	Hour	Summary of Events and Information	Remarks and references to Appendices
RENINGHELST	1/12/17	4 p.m.	"A" Section relieved "D" Section (5 guns at FITZCLARENCE FARM, 1 gun at STIRLING CASTLE), 2nd Lt. R. PRENTICE remained in charge.	
"	2/12/17		2nd Lt. H.R.V.H. HUNT returned from U.K.	
"	3/12/17		2nd Lt. A.J. O'REGAN proceeded to the line.	
"	4/12/17		"A" Section in the line, 2nd Lt. R.B. MORISON proceeded on leave to U.K.	
"	5/12/17		2nd Lt. R. PRENTICE returned from the line. Capt. E.E. WARD (1st Hants. Regt.) joined the Company and took over Command from Capt. H.K. BOYLE.	
"	6/12/17	4 p.m.	2nd Lt. W.H. CURTIS with "C" Section relieved "A" Section. No 44857 & Cpl. METHVEN, G.R. and No. 33016 Pte LYALL, W., awarded the Military Medal for gallant conduct on 26/11/17.	
"	7/12/17		2nd Lt. A. O'REGAN returned from the line.	
"	8/12/17		"C" Section in the line.	
"	9/12/17		2nd Lt. R. PRENTICE and 1 O.R. proceeded to IX Corps Gun School at BERTHEN.	
"	10/12/17		2nd Lt. H.R.V.H. HUNT proceeded to the line.	
"	11/12/17		Capt. E.E. WARD and 2nd Lt. R. PRENTICE (2nd Lt. W.H. CURTIS to guns) 226 Coy H.Q. relieved B9 H.Q. at STIRLING CASTLE; "D" Section (2nd Lt. H.R.V.H. HUNT to guns) relieved 6 guns of B9 M.G. Coy. near GHELUVELT.	
"	12/12/17	4:30 p.m.	B9 M.G. Coy relieved "C" Section in the line	
"	13/12/17	H.Q.+ "A" Section in the line		
"		H.Q.+ "B" Section in the line		
"		H.Q.+ "D" Section in the line		
"	14/12/17		2nd Lt. A. TO'Regan and 6 O.R. proceeded into the line.	
"	15/12/17	4 p.m.	"A" Section relieved "D" Section. 2nd Lt. R. PRENTICE returned to Camp.	
"	16/12/17		H.Q. and "A" Section in the line.	
"	17/12/17		Capt. H.K. BOYLE relieved Capt. E.E. WARD in the line.	
"	18/12/17		H.Q. + "A" Section in the line.	
"	19/12/17		Capt. E.E. WARD proceeded on leave to U.K. Capt. H.K. BOYLE assumed Command of the Company.	
"	20/12/17		2nd Lt. R.B. MORISON + 6 O.R. proceeded to the line.	
"	21/12/17	4 p.m.	"C" Section relieved "A" Section in the line. 2nd Lt. A. O'REGAN returned to Camp. 2nd Lt. W.H. CURTIS proceeded on leave to U.K.	

ORIGINAL

Army Form C. 2118.

WAR DIARY
or
INTELLIGENCE SUMMARY.
(Erase heading not required.)

Instructions regarding War Diaries and Intelligence Summaries are contained in F.S. Regs., Part II. and the Staff Manual respectively. Title pages will be prepared in manuscript.

Place	Date	Hour	Summary of Events and Information	Remarks and references to Appendices
RENINGHELST	22/12/17		HQ + "C" Section in the line.	
"	23/12/17		HQ + "C" Section in the line	
"	24/12/17		HQ + "C" Sections in the line	
"	25/12/17		HQ + "C" Sections in the line	
"	26/12/17	4pm	2nd Lt R. PRENTICE and "D" Section relieved 6 guns of 89 M.G. Coys in the line	
		5pm	89 M.G. Coy relieved. HQ (Capt H.K. BOYLE) and C Section (2nd Lt R.B. MORISON) in the line	
"	27/12/17		"D" Section in the line.	
"	28/12/17		"D" Section in the line. "B" Section (Lieut W.A. DOUST + 2nd Lt D.G. DIPLOCK + 35 O.R.) arrived from the Base.	
"	29/12/17		"D" Section in the line	
"	30/12/17		"D" Section in the line	
"	31/12/17	3pm	"A" Section (2nd Lt H.R.V.H. HUNT) relieved "D" Section (2nd Lt R. PRENTICE) in the line	

HK Boyle Capt
O.C. 226 M.G. Coy 1/1/18

"SECRET"

Vol 7

War Diary

of the 226th Company, Machine Gun Corps.

for the month of January 1918.

Volume. No. ____

(Sgd) _____ Capt.

D.A.A.G. 30th Division

WAR DIARY or INTELLIGENCE SUMMARY

Army Form C. 2118.

Place	Date	Hour	Summary of Events and Information	Remarks and references to Appendices
RENINGHELST	1/1/18		"A" Section in the line.	
"	2/1/18		" " " "	
"	3/1/18		" " " 2nd Lt R.B. MORISON & No.1. proceeded to "P" Battery T.15.d.	
"	"	4 p.m.	"C" Section relieved 90th M.G. Coy. at "P" Battery. One gun "A" Section at the Tower relieved by 89th M.G. Coy and relieved one gun of 90th M.G. Coy. at Clapham Junction. Company H.Q. relieved H.Q. 90th M.G. Coy at Stirling Castle.	
"	4/1/18		"H.Q." "A" and "C" Sections (10 guns) in the line. 2nd Lt D.G. DIPLOCK & 2 O.R. proceeded to B.V.E.S. Area as billeting party.	
"	5/1/18	8 p.m.	Company relieved in the line by 217th Machine Gun Coy.	
"	6/1/18	9 a.m.	Transport marched to BERTHEN (en route for BLARINGHAM)	
"	7/1/18	10.30 a.m.	Company marched to DICKEBUSCH, entrained 1 p.m., detrained with 2 SISLINGHAM 4.30 p.m. marched to BLARINGHAM arriving 7 p.m. Capt. E.E. WARD rejoined the Coy. & assumed command. 2nd Lt W.H. CURTIS rejoined from D.K.	
BLARINGHAM	8/1/18		In rest.	
"	9/1/18		In rest.	
"	10/1/18		In rest.	
"	11/1/18	3 a.m.	Company (with transport) marched to STEENBECQUE & entrained 9 p.m., detrained at LONGUEAU 11.30 p.m. and marched to HAMELET, arriving 11.30 p.m.	
HAMELET	12/1/18		In rest.	
"	13/1/18	8 a.m.	Company marched to HARBONNIÈRES	
HARBONNIÈRES	14/1/18		In rest.	
"	15/1/18		In rest.	
"	16/1/18		In rest.	
"	17/1/18		In rest.	
"	18/1/18	8 a.m.	Company marched to SAULCHOY. 2nd Lt R. PRENTICE & 3 wagons marched to FRETOY with stores.	
SAULCHOY	19/1/18	9.15 a.m.	Company marched to FRETOY. 2nd Lt R. PRENTICE & party marched to SAULCHOY to pick up stores	
FRETOY	20/1/18		Company at rest. 2 Lt R. PRENTICE & party returned.	
"	21/1/18		" "	
"	22/1/18		" "	

WAR DIARY or INTELLIGENCE SUMMARY

Army Form C. 2118.

Place	Date	Hour	Summary of Events and Information	Remarks and references to Appendices
FRETOY	23/1/18		Company in rest. 2nd Lt. R. PRENTICE proceeded to U.K. on leave.	
"	24/1/18		" " 11.30am Inspection by G.O.C., 30th Division. 2nd Lt. MORISON proceeded to BABOEUF	
"	25/1/18		" " with billeting party.	
"	26/1/18	9 a.m.	Company marched to BABOEUF. 2nd Lieut W.A. DOUST & 2nd Lt. A.T. O'REGAN proceeded to MARIZELE with billeting party.	
BABOEUF	27/1/18	9 a.m.	Company marched to MARIZELE. O.C. & 2nd i/c proceeded to the line at AMIGNY-ROUY and reconnoitred positions from French Cavalry Division preparatory to relieving. Made arrangements for taking over gun positions from French Cavalry Division on rejoining Company at MARIZELE, Lt. W.A. DOUST, 2nd Lt. D.G. DIPLOCK and 2nd Lt. A.T. O'REGAN with 12 mcs. proceeded into the line to take over 12 gun positions.	
"	28/1/18	5.30pm	2nd Lt R.B. MORISON with "A" Section and one Sub Section "B" relieved the French in the Rouy Sub Sector, guns being at B21d 10.50, B23c 53.55, B.23.c.60.45, B.23.c.60.45, B.23.c.60.d2 (2 guns) and B.29a 65.60. Sec. HQ at B22d 90.15. Regt. Head "C" Section + one Sub Section "B", joined 2nd Lt D.G. DIPLOCK & relieved the French, taking up gun positions 90D N.W. at B.29a 22.15 (2 guns), B28d 01.01, B34d 02.82, H.3a75.22, H.3a70.00, Sec. HQ. at H4.f 10.65. Advanced Coy. H.Q. with Lt. W.A. DOUST at Buff's HQ. at B.27.d 75.56. See Defence Scheme herewith.	
"	29/1/18		" " "A", "B" & "C" Sections in the line. 2pm 2nd Lt. A.T. O'REGAN returned to Read HQ.	
"	30/1/18		" " " " 2nd Lt. A.T. O'REGAN proceeded on leave to U.K.	
"	31/1/18		" " " O.C. reconnoitred positions for 4 guns in reserve near the BUTTES DE	
			ROUY.	

W.K. Boyle, Capt.
O.C. 226th Machine Gun Company

"Secret"

War Diary

of the 226th Company, Machine Gun Corps.

for the month of February 1918.

Volume No. 1.

Army Form C. 2118.

ORIGINAL

Instructions regarding War Diaries and Intelligence Summaries are contained in F.S. Regs., Part II. and the Staff Manual respectively. Title pages will be prepared in manuscript.

WAR DIARY
or
INTELLIGENCE SUMMARY.
(Erase heading not required.)

Place	Date	Hour	Summary of Events and Information	Remarks and references to Appendices
MARIZELE	1/2/18		Forward H.Q. + "A", "B" + "C" Sections in the line.	
"	2/2/18	5 a.m.	2nd Lt. H.R.V.H. HUNT with "D" Section proceeded into the line + were located at H.8.c.1.6.	
"	3/2/18		1 gun position sited at H.2.c.12.08, H.2.8.3.1, H.7h.8.5 and H.2.a.2.6.	
"	4/2/18		Forward H.Q. + 4 Sections in the line.	
"	5/2/18		" " O.C. + 2 other officers, 214 M.G. Coy, reconnoitred posn, gun positions	
			preparatory to taking over.	
			Guns re-organised in accordance with Divisional Defence Scheme 1 gun positions sited at:-	
			Left Sub-Sector Section HQ H.3.a.7.1. Reserve guns Supervision H.8, H.8.2.1.6.	
			1 B.23.d.1.1. 1 H.8.2.9.9.
			2 H.9.c.9.7. 2 H.9.8.5.4.
			3 H.3.c.8.8. 3 H.1.1.7.4.
			4 H.3.a.8.9. 4 H.9.d.9.9.
			6 H.3.a.6.2.	
			Right Sub-Section HQ	
			1 B.23.c.6.2.
			2 B.23.c.5.0.
			3 B.22.d.5.4.
			4 B.28.a.5.6.
			6 B.21.d.37.	
"	6/2/18	9am	and emplacements commenced.	
			Company HQ moved into Shelter trench together with "E" a working party consisting of 1 NCO available manual	
			Details Coy. (Capt E.E. WARD + 6/Lt H.R. BOYLE)	
"	7/2/18		Company in the Line.	
"	8/2/18		" " "	
"	9/2/18	10.30pm	Company relieved in the line by 214 M.G. Coy. and marched to BOURGUIGNON.	
BOURGUIGNON	10/2/18		Company marched to GUISCARD. 2nd Lt. R. PRENTICE rejoined from leave to U.K.	
GUISCARD	11/2/18		Company marched to ESMERY HALLON. The four M.G. Coys of the Division formed	
			into 30th Divl. M.G. Training Group.	
ESMERY-HALLON	12/2/18		Coy at rest.	
"	13/2/18		Company inspected near LIBREMONT by the Commander-in-Chief.	

ORIGINAL

Army Form C. 2118.

Instructions regarding War Diaries and Intelligence Summaries are contained in F. S. Regs., Part II. and the Staff Manual respectively. Title pages will be prepared in manuscript.

WAR DIARY
or
INTELLIGENCE SUMMARY.
(Erase heading not required.)

Place	Date	Hour	Summary of Events and Information	Remarks and references to Appendices
ESMERY-HALLON	14.2.18		Training under Battalion arrangements	
"	15.2.18		Capt. H.K. BOYLE & 3 O.R. proceeded to CAMIERS for course at S.A. School. 1 O.R. proceeded to U.K. on leave. Lt. W.A. DOUST assumed the duties of Observer in aeroplane.	
"	16.2.18		Capt. E.E. WARD, 2/Lt. D.G. DIPLOCK, 2/Lt. R. PRENTICE & 4 O.R. went up the line to reconnoitre the Battle zone. Lt. A. McCOLL proceeded to U.K. on leave.	
"	17.2.18		1 O.R. attached temp 11 S. Coys. returned to their unit. Capt. E.E. WARD proceeded to HAM for Corps Conference.	
"	18.2.18		2 D.R. to Field Ambulance. Lt. W.A. DOUST assumed duties of O.C. Coy. 4 O.R. proceeded to HAM for interment & returned same day. 1 O.R. 4/5 7.A. 2/Lt. R.B. MORISON & 10 O.R. returned from C.C.S. 1 O.R. rejoined from leave.	
"	19.2.18		Training under Battalion arrangements.	
"	20.2.18		2/Lt A.J. O'REGAN & 10 O.R. proceeded to DOUCHY as billeting party. 1 O.R. proceeded to FRETOY for Church-party course. 10 O.R. to F.A. Capt. E.E. WARD returned from Conference at HAM & reassumed duties of O.C. Coy.	
"	21.2.18		Company marched to DOUCHY.	
DOUCHY	22.2.18		Company employed all day constructing cover for men & horses.	
"	23.2.18		Coy employed as above yesterday. Kit inspection afternoon. 1 O.R. to F.A. 2/Lt A.J. O'Regan assumed the duties of Battalion Intelligence Officer. Capt. E.E. WARD proceeded to HAM to reconnoitre.	
"	24.2.18	morning	'A' Section (2/Lt MORISON) 'B' Section (2/Lt PRENTICE) ('C' Section (2/Lt D. PLOCK) with 12 gun took up positions in Battle Zone. A* 1+2 guns A13 G-15.50 B F11070.48 9.10 F4G 90.10	
			Ref Sheets 66D N.E. 3+4 — F182.10.45 7+8 F11250.43 11.12 F4G 85.15	
			+ 66 C.N.W.	
		after noon	Capt E.E. WARD, Lt W.A. DOUST & 2/Lt A.R.V.HUNT proceeded to Battle zone to reconnoitre positions for remaining 4 guns	

ORIGINAL

WAR DIARY or INTELLIGENCE SUMMARY

Army Form C. 2118.

(Erase heading not required.)

Place	Date	Hour	Summary of Events and Information	Remarks and references to Appendices
DOUCHY	25.2.18		2/Lt W.T. HOWARTH + 5 O.R. joined company from Reinforcement Camp. Capt E.E. WARD + 2 EVAN.D.DUST mounted 12 guns in the Battle Zone.	
"	26.2.18	8 am	2/Lt H.R.N.H. HUNT ordered to take up position in Battle Zone with 4 guns.	G.1025 – 51.75. 55.64 Ret Shelt – 26.51.76. 10.17D – 27.F.92c. 15.05. 55.D.N.E. – 28.F.86. 30.23 ──
		5.45 pm	4 guns reported in action.	10 R. returned from Y.A.
			12 guns in the line, 4 in reserve – work going on at all 16 positions.	
"	27.2.18		Capt. E.E. WARD visited guns in Battle Zone. 10 R.G. F.A. 18 attacked infantry when juniors Coy.	
"	28.2.18	Morning	Capt. WARD + Lt. DOUST VISITED Battle Zone. 4 O.R. joined Coy. from Base.	
		Evening	2/Lt HUNT (D Section) relieved 4 guns of 21st Coy. 13+14 guns F4a 35.45 – 15+16 F4a 55.65 H.Q. moved to ETREILLERS. Capt WARD assumed command of 24 guns in Battle Zone – 16 guns of 226th Coy + 8 guns of 21st Coy. 17+18 X28c 15.875. Location of Battle Zone guns H.Q. X27c 40.15	19+20 X28a 80.20 21+22 X23c 10.88 23+24 X25a 20.01

W.A. Dewar
Lieut.
O.C. 226th M.G. Coy

www.ingramcontent.com/pod-product-compliance
Lightning Source LLC
Chambersburg PA
CBHW081505160426
43193CB00014B/2594